W9-CKL-740

The 50 States

Written by Patricia Levy
Illustrated by Mike White

p

This is a Parragon Publishing Book
This edition published in 2002

Parragon Publishing
Queen Street House
4 Queen Street
Bath BA1 1HE, UK

ISBN 0-75259-154-1

Printed in China.

Produced by
Monkey Puzzle Media Ltd

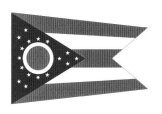

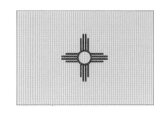

Contents

The United States

ALASKA

CANADA

PACIFIC OCEAN

CANADA

WASHINGTON

MONTANA

OREGON

IDAHO

WYOMING

NEVADA

UTAH

COLORA

CALIFORNIA

ARIZONA

NEW MEXICO

PACIFIC OCEAN

MEXICO

U.S. Facts

Area: 3,716,830 sq miles (9,629,091 sq km)

Population: 272,639,608

Length of coastline: 12,373 miles (19,924 km)

Highest point: Mt McKinley, Alaska 20,320 feet (6,194 meters)

Lowest point: Death Valley, California −282 feet (−86 meters)

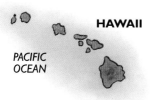

HAWAII

PACIFIC OCEAN

KEY TO THE MAPS OF THE 50 STATES

☐ **National capital (Washington, D.C.)**

■ **State capitals**

● **Other main cities**

Hawaii and Alaska are not shown at the same scale as the rest of the U.S.

4

Capital Facts

Area of District of Columbia:
67 sq miles (173.5 sq km)

Population: Washington 607,000
Residential area 5,689,263

The Capitol building and the Washington
Monument in Washington, D.C.

NEW
HAMPSHIRE

VERMONT   MAINE

NEW YORK

NORTH
DAKOTA

MINNESOTA

MICHIGAN

MASSACHUSETTS

WISCONSIN

SOUTH
DAKOTA

RHODE
ISLAND

PENNSYLVANIA

CONNECTICUT

IOWA

OHIO

NEW JERSEY

NEBRASKA

INDIANA

DELAWARE

ILLINOIS

WEST
VIRGINIA

MARYLAND

VIRGINIA

WASHINGTON, D.C.

KANSAS

MISSOURI

KENTUCKY

NORTH
CAROLINA

TENNESSEE

OKLAHOMA   ARKANSAS

SOUTH
CAROLINA

GEORGIA

ALABAMA

ATLANTIC OCEAN

TEXAS

MISSISSIPPI   FLORIDA

LOUISIANA

GULF OF MEXICO

5

What lay dormant for 130 years before waking up in 1980?

THE ALREADY GRUMBLING VOLCANO MOUNT ST HELENS. ON MAY 18, 1980 this peak in the Cascade mountains in Washington erupted when a severe earthquake opened a crack along its side. The side of the mountain blew out and debris, lava, and ash spread out in a 17 mile (27 km) arc, flattening forests in its path. Thirty people were killed and the height of the mountain 8,229 ft (2,508 m) was reduced by 1,312 ft (400 m).

How did the first families to cross the continent meet a disastrous end?

Marcus Whitman, his wife Narcissa, the Rev. Henry Spalding, and his wife made the first wagon train crossing that included women. They built a mission at Waiilatpu, and helped other families make the crossing after them. But in 1874 they and 12 other people were killed by Native Americans.

Where can you see a phantom ship sailing across a volcano?

In Crater Lake National Park, southwestern Oregon. A lake has formed in the crater of an extinct volcano. The lake is surrounded by cliffs 500—2,000 ft (150—600 m) high. At the southern end is a mass of lava, which looks like a ship under sail.

Who were the first Europeans to sight Oregon?

Probably Spanish sailors in the 1500s. The headland of the Columbia River was given the name Cape Disappointment because explorers could not find the river mouth. In 1792 it was discovered by Robert Gray who named it after his ship, the *Columbia*.

Where does a snake run into hell?

The Snake River runs through Idaho. It cuts through the Rocky Mountains in the west of the United States at Hell's Canyon. This is the deepest gorge in North America at 7,776 ft (2,370 m). It is part of the Hell's Canyon Wilderness, a National Park.

Crater Lake is the second deepest lake in North America.

CANADA
WASHINGTON
Seattle
Spokane
Olympia
Portland
MONTANA
Salem
OREGON
Boise
Idaho Falls
IDAHO
CALIFORNIA
NEVADA
UTAH
WYOMING
Pacific Ocean

Washington

Oregon

Idaho

Which is the apple state?

The area of Washington to the west of the Cascade mountain range has some of the thickest forests in the world. It is also one of the wettest areas in the U.S., and this makes the area good for growing produce. In fact, Washington grows more apples than any other state in the United States. East of the Cascade Range there is little rain and few trees.

Why did Lewis and Clarke go up-river?

Lewis and Clarke were the two men chosen by President Thomas Jefferson in 1804 to explore the land west of the Mississippi. They took a small party and followed the Missouri River to its source, crossed the continental divide and then found and followed the Columbia River. Their expedition gave America its claim to the Oregon territories.

How did Idaho get its unusual shape?

ON THE MAP IDAHO IS SHAPED LIKE A PLATFORM BOOT WITH A large, almost square section in the south but an odd north-south section. Idaho was created after the six states and one Canadian province that surround it had created their borders. It is a strip of land that no one else claimed. The surrounding settlers would have acted differently, had they realized what a wealth of silver, zinc, lead, and lumber Idaho would eventually give up!

Where can you see salmon climbing a ladder?

The Columbia River in Washington has been dammed in several places and this makes it impossible for salmon to reach their breeding grounds. So at Bonneville Dam a special ladder has been built where the salmon can jump in stages up the height of the dam.

Which Seattle-born businessman is mega-rich?

Bill Gates of the Microsoft Corporation. He made his first billion at the age of 31 after inventing the MS-DOS system and then Windows. Today he is one of the richest men in the world.

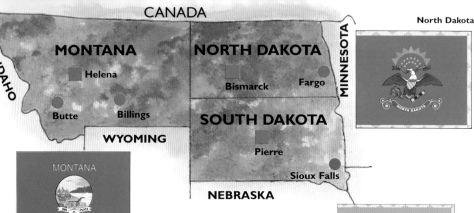

CANADA

MONTANA

Helena

Butte · Billings

WYOMING

NORTH DAKOTA

Bismarck · Fargo

MINNESOTA

SOUTH DAKOTA

Pierre

Sioux Falls

NEBRASKA

IDAHO

Montana

North Dakota

South Dakota

Why is Montana named the Bonanza State?

MONTANA HAS MANY NICKNAMES, INCLUDING BIG SKY COUNTRY, Land of the Shining Mountains, and the Treasure State. It's called Bonanza because of its wealth of natural resources. Montana has huge stretches of fertile soil suitable for wheat and grassland for grazing. It has valuable minerals and millions of acres of timber, particularly spruce, larch, and pine, all fast-growing and very good for commercial use. Another major resource is its beautiful scenery, which attracts thousands of tourists each year.

What was Custer's Last Stand?

In 1874 gold prospectors flooded into South Dakota regardless of the understandably hostile Sioux whose land it was. General Custer was part of the force sent to protect the prospectors. In 1876, disobeying orders, he led his troops into an ambush by 6,000 Native Americans at Little Bighorn. He and all 200 of his soldiers were killed. This event was named Custer's Last Stand.

What are the Badlands?

An area of North and South Dakota where erosion has carved strange shapes out of the rock and there is no vegetation. Pioneers named it the Badlands because it was so difficult to cross. In places, underground lignite (brown coal) fires have melted the rock and created a mass of striking colors. The remains of saber-toothed tigers have been found there.

To the east of Montana, the Great Plains stretch for miles; to the west the Rockies tower over the land.

Who was Calamity Jane?

Martha Jane Canary, born 1852. She lived in Virginia City and was a very good horsewoman. She drove freight wagons for a time and then went to Deadwood in South Dakota during the gold rush of 1864. Many stories tell of her exploits, including how she fought Native Americans, wore men's clothes, and got very drunk.

Calamity Jane was born in Princeton, Missouri. She is said to have promised "calamity" to any man who tried to court her… but in 1885 she got married!

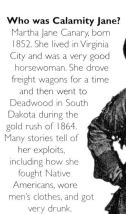

Why is "big" an important word for Alaska?

WHEN ALASKA JOINED THE UNION IT INCREASED THE size of the U.S. by a fifth. It brought with it some big facts. It has 28,000 miles (44,800 km) of glaciers; the highest mountain in North America (Mount McKinley); the largest carnivorous land mammal (the kodiac bear); and part of the longest navigable waterway in the world (the Yukon River).

Where can you find the second longest mountain chain in the world?

The Rocky Mountains, Montana. They begin far north of Montana in Alaska, cross Canada, and dominate the western third of the United States, but their main bulk is in Montana. Granite Peak is the highest mountain in the state at 12,799 ft (3,840 m).

Where is "the richest hill on Earth"?

At Butte, Montana. In 1881 a prospector, Marcus Daly, who was searching for silver, found copper instead. The town of Butte grew up quickly and soon turned into a lawless place with bandits controlling the roads. Daly's Anaconda Company became one of the biggest mining companies in the world.

Where would you find the world's tallest manmade structure?

Surprisingly, not in New York City but in North Dakota where the KTHI-TV mast is 2,063 ft (619 m) high. It is supported by guy wires and would not stand up on its own. For the tallest self-supporting structure, you would have to go to Toronto in Canada.

Alaska

ALASKA

Barrow

Fairbanks

Anchorage

Juneau

CANADA

Pacific Ocean

John Wayne is possibly the most famous cowboy-actor in the world.

Who added his own bad name to the English language?

In 1950 Joseph McCarthy, the senator for Wisconsin, claimed he had a list of communists employed by the State Department. The Senate Committee for un-American activities began investigations into communist activity within government. Many people in the film industry were ruined by the investigations, although no accusations were ever proved. Finally McCarthy went too far and accused President Eisenhower of being a communist. The word "McCarthyism" now means the persecution of innocent people with unproved charges.

How does Minnesota take care of its wildlife?

Minnesota has vast resources of forest and was once a major logging center. Recently, Minnesota has set aside more land for wildlife preservation than any other state. In several areas where trees were cut down, the forest has been replanted.

Who created the famous cartoon Peanuts?

Charles M. Schultz. He was born in Minneapolis, Minnesota, in 1922 and invented the cartoon strip Peanuts in 1950. It was originally named Li'l Folks, but has always included the beagle dog Snoopy and his owner Charlie Brown. It is the most successful cartoon strip in the world.

Why did Marian Morrison change names?

Marian became one of Iowa's most famous citizens, starring in films such as Stagecoach (1939), True Grit (1969), The Alamo (1960) and many more. He was in fact John Wayne, born in Winterset, Iowa, in 1907. He changed his name, for obvious reasons, in the 1930s.

Which is America's cheesiest state?

Wisconsin has been America's leading producer of milk since 1920, and today has about 1,750,000 cows. The first cheese factory was opened there in 1864 and Wisconsin cheese is internationally renowned. The state also has many creameries and butter factories.

How did wheat from Iowa make bread in Moscow?

IOWA PRODUCES MASSES OF GRAIN—OVER A BILLION TONS IN SOME YEARS. IN THE 1950s the rest of the U.S. bought little of this harvest and Iowa farmers began to suffer. Then Soviet premier Kruschev visited Iowa and set up a trade link between Iowa and Russia. The trade earned the state a huge annual revenue and it came to depend on it. In 1979 there was a trade embargo (ban) following the Afghanistan war, but the link was re-established in 1981.

How did a Gumm become a Garland?
Filmstar Judy Garland (1922—69) was born in Grand Rapids, Minnesota, although she didn't spend much of her time there. Her real name was Frances Gumm and she worked as a child performer in her parents' singing act before being spotted by Louis B. Mayer of MGM studios.

Where is the birthplace of the artist formerly known as Prince?
Prince Rogers Nelson was born in Minneapolis on June 7th 1959. By the age of 12 he was playing in a band. He went on to produce songs such as *Purple Rain*, and the soundtrack to *Batman*. In 1993 he changed his name to a symbol made up of the two biological signs for male and female.

How do people enjoy Wisconsin's great outdoors?
Hunting is the most popular sporting activity in Wisconsin—for bear, game birds, and deer. The vast areas of lakeland offer fishing —especially for the curiously named muskellunge—and watersports of many kinds. In winter there are iceboat races on Lake Winnebago.

CANADA

Lake Superior

N. DAKOTA

S. DAKOTA

NEBRASKA

Duluth

MICHIGAN

MINNESOTA

St Paul

WISCONSIN

Minneapolis

Lake Michigan

Madison

Milwaukee

IOWA

ILLINOIS

OHIO

Des Moines

MISSOURI

Wisconsin

Iowa

Minnesota

11

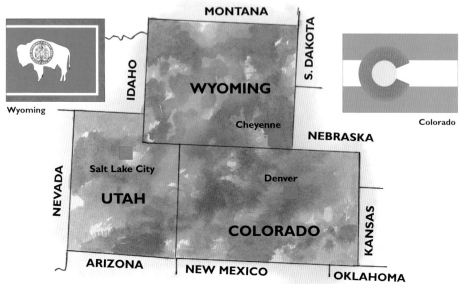

MONTANA

WYOMING

S. DAKOTA

IDAHO

Cheyenne

NEBRASKA

NEVADA

Salt Lake City

UTAH

Denver

COLORADO

KANSAS

ARIZONA

NEW MEXICO

OKLAHOMA

Wyoming

Colorado

Utah

What is the Rainbow Bridge?

THE RAINBOW BRIDGE IS THE WORLD'S LARGEST NATURAL BRIDGE, FOUND in a national park in southeastern Utah. It is a salmon pink sandstone arch 309 ft (93 m) high and 278 ft (84 m) wide. Native Americans once considered it a sacred site. The first white men saw it in 1909.

What is the Devil's Tower?

Sixty million years ago in northeastern Wyoming, molten lava forced its way up through sandstone rock and gradually cooled. Over the millennia the sandstone was eroded until all that remained was the Devil's Tower—a fluted column of volcanic rock standing 865 ft (260 m) high above the trees.

Which religious group founded Utah?

In 1847 Utah was Native American land. Then a religious group named the Mormons, persecuted in the East because the men of the sect took several wives, settled near Salt Lake and founded the state. Their leader, Brigham Young, became governor of the state. Even today, more than 70 percent of the people living in Utah are Mormons.

Arches National Park

Where can you sit on the Great White Throne?

In Southern Utah the Virgin River has formed a canyon between huge sheer-walled sandstone cliffs. A Mormon scout was the first white man to discover the place in 1858. Set into the east wall inside the canyon is a natural structure that looks like a massive chair, and is named the Great White Throne. The area is very beautiful and is now a national park.

Which Wild West state first gave women the vote?

Wyoming is famous for its Wild West stories of cattle ranchers and wagon trains. Its pioneers were fur traders who fought the Native Americans and took their territory. One of Wyoming's best known frontiersmen was Buffalo Bill Cody, who founded the town of Cody. Wyoming is named the Equality State, because in 1869 it was the first state to give women the vote and to allow them to stand for public office. The first woman governor in the United States was Nellie Taloe Ross, elected in Wyoming in 1929.

What do Esther, Spotted Tail, Robert and John have in common?

They are all famous citizens of Wyoming, Utah, and California. Wyoming's Esther Morris was an important figure in the women's suffrage movement—in 1870 she became the first American woman to be made a justice of the peace. Spotted Tail was a Wyoming Sioux chief who for a long time preserved his nation's territory and avoided war with white men. Among Utah's famous are Robert Redford, born in California but now living in a Utah ski resort. Colorado was home to John Denver, the singer and songwriter known for songs such as *Windsong* and *Leaving on a Jet Plane.*

Which was the world's first national park?

YELLOWSTONE NATIONAL PARK, STRETCHING ACROSS WYOMING, Idaho, and Montana, was established in 1872. It was the first protected area for wildlife in the world. Here you can see the geyser named Old Faithful, the hot springs, the Yellowstone Falls, rock formations, and herds of wild buffalo.

Where can you find a palace inside a cliff?

At Mesa Verde, Colorado, which has the best preserved cliff dwellings in America. The steep hill is riddled with more than 600 cave dwellings. One of these is known as the Cliff Palace and has 223 rooms. The cliff was inhabited from early Christian times.

Which is the highest city in the U.S.?

Denver, the capital city of Colorado. Denver is the gateway to the Rocky Mountains, which dominate the western half of the state. It calls itself the "Mile High City." Eight hundred of Colorado's mountains are above 14,223 ft (4,334 m) high.

Where is the lowest point in the western hemisphere?

Straddling the border between California and Nevada is Death Valley. It is a deep trough between two mountain ranges and 550 sq miles (330 sq km) of it lie 286 ft (86 m) below sea level. It is the lowest, and also the hottest, place in the western hemisphere.

Which U.S. state produces the most gold?

Since the Comstock Lode was discovered in 1859 Nevada has been a major producer of both gold and silver. The lode ran out after about 20 years but many smaller deposits have since been found. Today, mining for gold, silver, barite, mercury, lithium, and gemstones is one of Nevada's most important industries.

Which state has the grisliest criminal record?

California has the largest prison population of the U.S. with 153,010 inmates, the highest number of murders (2,916 in 1996), and the most prisoners (both men and women) on death row (454 in 1996). Incidentally, the U.S. has the largest prison population in the world.

Where can you find the largest and tallest living thing on Earth?

In CALIFORNIA, OF COURSE.

The General Sherman giant sequoia tree in Sequoia National Park is 280 ft (85 m) high and weighs an estimated 2,461 tons.

General Sherman
Giant Sequoia

California

Which state is the top of the pops?

Ever since California was admitted to the union in 1850, it has had the highest population growth rate of the U.S. In the beginning, it had a population of 10,000. By 1940, less than a century later, its population was 7 million! By 1970, California had more people than any other state in the U.S., and it has remained the most populated ever since. Los Angeles County alone has more citizens than at least 40 of the other states! Nowadays the population of California stands at just under 30 million.

IDAHO

Nevada

NEVADA

UTAH

Las Vegas

ARIZONA

MEXICO

San Francisco's Golden Gate Bridge was built in 1937.

What is Methuselah doing in Nevada?
Methuselah is the pet name of a giant bristlecone pine tree growing on Wheeler Peak, Nevada. It is thought to be the oldest living tree in America at around 4,900 years old.

What sort of chips can you find in Santa Clara?
In the 1970s and 1980s a large number of electronics companies settled in the Santa Clara Valley, an area southwest of San Francisco. It later became known as Silicon Valley after the material that computer chips are made of.

Where can you visit a prison in a park?
At the Golden Gate National Park near San Francisco. The park includes shoreline, redwood forests, the National Maritime Museum and the island of Alcatraz. Alcatraz served as a maximum security prison from 1933 to 1963. Native Americans reclaimed it for a time in 1968.

Where is the driest place in the U.S.?

What exploded at Frenchman's Flat and Yucca Flat?
Because Nevada has so few people, it has been used as a nuclear weapons test site. Frenchman's Flat and Yucca Flat, remote areas of southern Nevada, were used for exploding atomic bombs in 1951. In 1961 nuclear testing was banned, but in 1968 more nuclear weapons were exploded in Nevada, this time 3,800 ft (1,158 m) underground.
Nuclear reactor research also began in Nevada—at the Las Vegas Bombing and Gunnery Range.

NEVADA HAS THE LOWEST RAINFALL OF ANY STATE OF THE UNION. ONLY about 9 in (23 cm) of rain falls every year in the northeast, while around Las Vegas they get less than 4 in (10 cm). The state is dominated by the Sierra Nevada, which rises along its western border and cuts off the damp winds that blow eastwards from the Pacific Ocean.

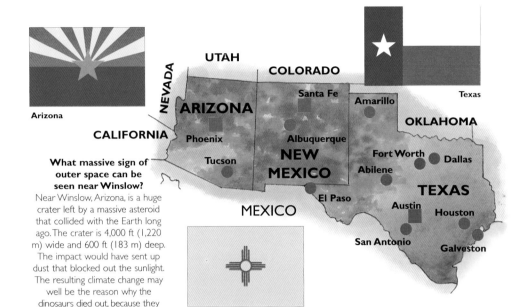

Arizona

New Mexico

Texas

UTAH
COLORADO
NEVADA
ARIZONA
CALIFORNIA
Santa Fe
Amarillo
Texas
OKLAHOMA
Phoenix
Albuquerque
Tucson
NEW
MEXICO
Fort Worth
Dallas
Abilene
MEXICO
El Paso
Austin
San Antonio
TEXAS
Houston
Galveston

What massive sign of outer space can be seen near Winslow?

Near Winslow, Arizona, is a huge crater left by a massive asteroid that collided with the Earth long ago. The crater is 4,000 ft (1,220 m) wide and 600 ft (183 m) deep. The impact would have sent up dust that blocked out the sunlight. The resulting climate change may well be the reason why the dinosaurs died out, because they depended for their food on plants that could no longer grow.

Who was William Bonney?

Billy the Kid. He was born in New York but moved to New Mexico as a child. He led a band of outlaws and claimed to have killed 27 men. Billy the Kid escaped from jail while awaiting execution and in 1881, aged 22, he was gunned down by Pat Garrett.

Where can you travel on the Devil's Road to see living organ pipes and Gila monsters?

One of Arizona's many strange habitats is the Organ Pipe Cactus National Monument, a park on the Mexican border. Here the rare organ pipe cactus grows to a height of 20 ft (6 m). The poisonous Gila monster, a type of lizard, also thrives here. A route across the Arizona desert was created around 1700 by Father Eusebio Kino, who named it El Camino del Diablo, the Devil's Road. It was a punishing route and many of the pioneers who used it died on the crossing.

What sent up a mushroom cloud at White Sands?

LOS ALAMOS IN NEW MEXICO WAS ONE OF AMERICA'S FIRST NUCLEAR WEAPONS research stations and the first atomic bomb in the world was assembled there. In 1945 the world's first nuclear weapon was detonated at White Sands, New Mexico.

White Sands, New Mexico

Why do Texans remember the Alamo?
In 1836, during the war for independence from Mexico, the Alamo, a fort in San Antonio, was occupied by 180 Americans. It was besieged by thousands of Mexican troops and every American was killed. The Texan war cry from that day was: "Remember the Alamo!"

Davy Crocket was one of the Texans besieged at the Alamo.

Where are the world's largest underground labyrinths?
The Carlsbad Caverns under the Guadelupe Mountains in New Mexico are 46,755 acres (20,000 hectares) of caves with stunning stalactites and stalagmites. 21 miles (33 km) of labyrinth have so far been explored.

What is Sky City?
An ancient site of pueblo ruins and cliff dwellings in Cibola County, New Mexico. Multi-roomed houses have been built into the caves in a sheer cliff 337 ft (101 m) high. The dwellings have mud-walled rooms—and are still inhabited today by the Acoma people.

How did a computer grow out of a radio shack?
The Tandy Corporation, based in Forth Worth, Texas, grew out of an electrical chain store named Radio Shack. In 1977 Tandy developed an affordable personal computer, the Altair 800. It was the first computer to have a keyboard like the ones used today.

What plants and animals thrive in the desert?

ARIZONA, NEW MEXICO AND TEXAS HAVE RARE DESERT PLANTS. A hundred species of cacti thrive here, as does the mesquite bush, a small spiny tree of the pea family. The agave and its close relation the yucca are tall plants that preserve water in their fleshy, waxy leaves. The creosote bush, as its name implies, has leaves that give off a strong smell of creosote. Animal life is varied too—there are coyotes, mountain lions, wildcats, and various deer as well as scorpions, rattlesnakes, and lots of birds.

How many flags have flown over Texas?
Six! From 1519 to 1685 it was Spanish. In 1685 France claimed it for a short time, then in 1691 Spain retrieved it. Mexico was the next state to claim sovereignty, then from 1836 to 1845 it was independent. In 1845 it joined the union—but from 1861 to 1865 it was part of the confederacy!

Kansas

Nebraska

Oklahoma

Why would you recognize Scott's Bluff and Chimney Rock?

Because they are famous landmarks on the old Oregon Trail, and have appeared in hundreds of westerns. Chimney Rock is a sandstone pinnacle near the Platte River in Nebraska. Pioneer groups often camped beside it. Scott's Bluff in the west of Nebraska is a cliff 800 ft (244 m) tall. The Pony Express passed by it.

Where are the Glass Mountains?

Near Fairview in Oklahoma, the mountains are covered in tiny selenite crystals, which from a distance makes them sparkle like glass. This is why they are known as the Glass Mountains, or sometimes the Gloss Mountains.

What is Arbor Day?

When the pioneers arrived in Nebraska they discovered that there were very few trees. Arbor Day (the name comes from the Latin for tree) was invented by J. Sterling Morton, a journalist who later became Secretary for Agriculture. On the very first Arbor Day in 1872 over a million trees were planted—Nebraska's present-day forests owe their existence largely to this day.

Why is Oklahoma the Sooner State?

FOR 50 YEARS OKLAHOMA WAS BANNED TO WHITE SETTLERS. IT WAS SET ASIDE as an area for the Native Americans who had chosen not to fight the white people who took their land. At that time Oklahoma was called Indian Territory. But in 1889 the government decided to break their agreement and open up the land for white settlers. Lots of settlers could not wait for the official date, so to get their hands on the best land they moved in sooner than was allowed. Hence the name.

Where can you see dinosaur footprints?

In the west of Oklahoma is an area known as the panhandle, a little strip of land that sticks out along the northern border of Texas. This area has the biggest range of dinosaur fossils in America. In creek beds here you can see dinosaur footprints made 200 million years ago.

How did Turkey Red transform the Great Plains?

THE GREAT PLAINS ARE THE RICH FARMING LANDS OF OKLAHOMA, Kansas, and Nebraska. But their very dry summers often meant that farmers lost all their crops to drought. When Mennonite settlers from Russia arrived in the Great Plains, they brought with them a special hardy type of wheat named Turkey Red. The Russian wheat was tough enough to survive the winter in the Great Plains—it could be planted in autumn and was ready to harvest before the drought set in. By the early 1900s Turkey Red was the main crop in the Great Plains.

Who were the Okies?
These were the Oklahoman farmers who were driven off their land by the great dust bowl—a combination of drought and winds that reduced the land to whirling dust where nothing would grow. The poverty-stricken families trekked across America to find work—but the economic depression made their task very difficult.

What started the American Civil War?
The American Civil War was caused mainly by a quarrel over slavery. The war lasted from 1861 to 1865 and was fought between the northern and the southern states of the U.S.. The economy of the southern states relied on black slaves shipped from Africa to work in the cotton plantations and on the farms of wealthy white owners. The northern states knew that slavery was wrong, and wanted it banned. A law named the Kansas Nebraska Act, passed in 1854, said that these two southern states could decide if they wanted slavery or not. This caused an almighty row to blow up, which eventually resulted in civil war.

Why were the five civilized tribes cruelly treated?
The Cherokees, Creeks, Choctaws, Chickasaws, and Seminoles were named "civilized" by European settlers because they agreed to the white man taking their lands, adopted white customs, and learned to read and write. In exchange for giving up their rich homelands to the whites, they were given a barren area—Oklahoma. They settled there and managed to survive. But when the whites saw the land could be lived on after all, they changed their minds. In 1889 they claimed most of Oklahoma too, pushing the "civilized" tribes into even smaller tracts of land.

Many people were forced to pack up their homes and move on to find work.

Who shed blood at Gettysberg?

IN 1863 GETTYSBURG WAS THE SCENE OF THE BLOODIEST BATTLE OF THE American Civil War. Confederacy troops from the southern states invaded Union territory and threatened the crossroads town of Gettysburg in Pennsylvania. 28,000 Confederate men and 23,000 Union soldiers from the northern states were killed or wounded. The battle took three days, and though the Confederates came close to winning, in the end they lost both the battle and the war.

How much did Peter Minuit pay for Manhattan?
When Peter Minuit arrived in America in 1626 Manhattan Island was occupied by the Wappinger Native Americans. He traded the island for some trinkets—worth about $24. The Wappinger thought they were selling the right to share the island—but the tricksy Dutch settler insisted it was a purchase.

Which state has more professional sports teams than any other in America?
Pennsylvania, with seven professional sports teams. They are the Philadelphia Phillies and Pittsburgh Pirates in baseball, the 76ers in basketball, the Pittsburgh Steelers and Philadelphia Eagles in football, and an ice hockey team—the Pittsburgh Penguins.

What was the first capital of the United States?
New York. During the War of Independence New York was one of the leading states. It was the 11th state to ratify the constitution. George Washington's inauguration ceremony took place in New York.

Where were America's first department stores?
Pennsylvania. John Wanamaker opened America's first department store in the 1870s in Philadelphia. Later, Frank Woolworth opened his five-and-ten-cent stores in Lancaster. Other chain stores were also founded in Pennsylvania—Kress, Kresge, Newberry's, and Grants.

Who was America's first woman doctor?
When Elizabeth Blackwell decided to become a doctor, she could not get a school to accept her because she was a woman, and so she studied privately. Eventually the Geneva Medical School in western New York recognized her abilities and enrolled her. She graduated top of her class in 1849.

Manhattan is a center of broadcasting, publishing, and entertainment.

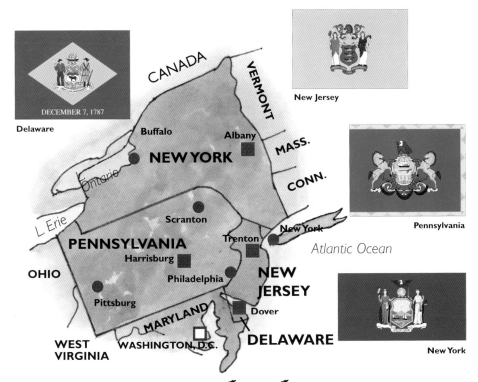

Delaware

DECEMBER 7, 1787

New Jersey

Pennsylvania

New York

CANADA

VERMONT

Buffalo

Albany

MASS.

NEW YORK

CONN.

L. Ontario

Scranton

L. Erie

PENNSYLVANIA

Trenton

New York

Atlantic Ocean

Harrisburg

OHIO

Philadelphia

NEW JERSEY

Pittsburg

Dover

MARYLAND

WEST VIRGINIA

WASHINGTON, D.C.

DELAWARE

Where did knickerbockers first get together?

At Hoboken, New Jersey, during the first ever organized game of baseball! The game was invented in 1839 by a West Point cadet. It received its official set of rules in 1845 when the Knickerbocker Baseball Club of New York City was founded. In 1846 the New York Knickerbockers played their historic first game against the Hoboken Knickerbocker Giants.

Which state is almost completely surrounded by water?

New Jersey! Well over 90 per cent of its border is water. The Delaware River forms its western border, Delaware Bay and the Atlantic lie to the south, while its northeastern border follows the Hudson River. Only 50 miles (80 km) of the state border is land—where it joins with New York.

What have Morse Code, the light bulb, and the submarine got in common?

THEY WERE ALL INVENTED IN NEW JERSEY. IN 1838 SAMUEL B. MORSE, AN ARTIST BY training, patented the first magnetic telegraph. The line ran from Washington to Baltimore, New Jersey, and the first transmitted message read: "What hath God wrought?" Forty years later another New Jerseyman, Thomas Alva Edison, lit the first electric light bulb. In 1881 the New Jerseyman John P. Holland launched the first submarine. This and later submarines were double-hulled and carried jet-propelled torpedoes. Some of them were used in World War I.

Which state relies on lobsters and chickens?

MAINE IS REALLY FAMOUS FOR ITS DELICIOUS LOBSTERS—AND ITS broiler chickens are sold all around the United States. The chickens are reared and exported and the lobsters are pulled out of the waters of the Atlantic Ocean. Fishing has always been a big industry in Maine and the lobsters are one of the main reasons for that success.

What is a Rhode Island Red?

It's a chicken first bred in Rhode Island in 1895. The bird is very distinctive with red-brown feathers, and is equally valued for its eggs and its meat.

The Rhode Island Red was developed from Asian chickens.

Which teacher went into outer space?

She was a social studies teacher in Concord, New Hampshire, who in 1985 applied to become a member of the space shuttle team. She would have become the first teacher to go into outer space. But the shuttle *Challenger* exploded over the Atlantic Ocean a few seconds after take-off, killing everyone on board.

The Pilgrim Fathers landed at Cape Cod, Massachusetts, in 1620.

Which is America's oldest university?

Harvard University was founded in 1636 in Cambridge, Massachusetts. It is named after John Harvard, who donated books and money to the school. Harvard has an impressive list of ex-students, including John F. Kennedy, e.e. cummings, Robert Frost and T.S. Eliot, Janet Reno, Mary Robinson, and the actor Tommy Lee Jones.

Where is America's oldest synagogue?

It's the Touro Synagogue in Newport, Rhode Island, built between 1759 and 1763. From its earliest days Rhode Island was known for its tolerance of all religious faiths. The Touro Synagogue is now a national monument.

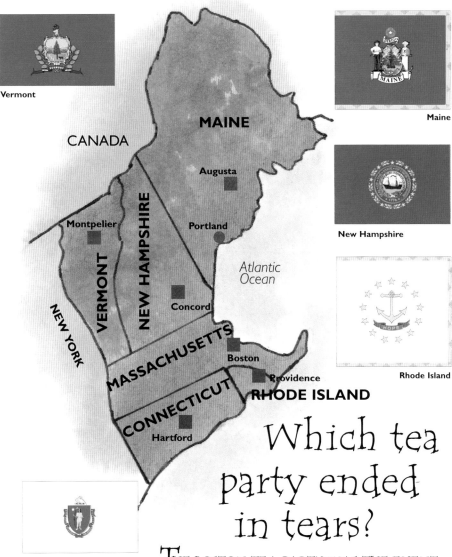

Vermont

MAINE

Maine

CANADA

Augusta

New Hampshire

Montpelier

Portland

VERMONT

NEW HAMPSHIRE

Atlantic Ocean

Concord

NEW YORK

Rhode Island

MASSACHUSETTS

Boston

CONNECTICUT

Providence

RHODE ISLAND

Hartford

Massachusetts

Connecticut

Which tea party ended in tears?

THE BOSTON TEA PARTY WAS THE EVENT THAT TRIGGERED THE WAR OF Independence. In 1773 Britain passed an act forcing American settlers to pay tax on tea to Britain. In protest, a group of men calling themselves the Sons of Liberty boarded the English ship *Dartmouth* in Boston Harbor. There they held a "tea party" by throwing its cargo of 342 chests of tea overboard. The British government responded with punishments against the state and very shortly afterwards war broke out between the British and the settlers.

Where was the first English settlement in America?

The Wrights' airplane was built in a bicycle factory.

THE VIRGINIA COMPANY OF LONDON SENT OUT THREE SHIPS TO ESTABLISH a colony in America and find something profitable to send back to England. In 1607 the sailors established Jamestown on Chesapeake Bay, Virginia. After three years of hardship they were ready to return home, but the colony was saved when its new governor, Lord De La Warr, arrived from England with supplies. In 1612 the settlers began tobacco farming, and from that time the colony thrived.

Who took to the air at Kill Devil Hills?
The first powered manned flight in the world took place in 1903 at Kill Devil Hills in North Carolina. The aircraft was built by the Wright brothers and had a gasoline engine, a propeller, and two parallel sets of wings. Orville Wright flew the plane while his brother Wilbur lay alongside the engine on the lower wing. The plane flew 120 ft (36 m).

Which state heard the first gunshots of the Civil War?
On December 20, 1860, South Carolina seceded from the Union. It was the first state to drop out. Ten others followed. The first shots of the Civil War were fired in South Carolina by Confederate troops.

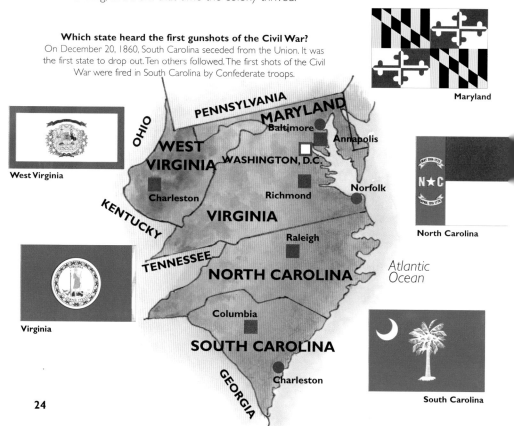

Maryland

West Virginia

North Carolina

Virginia

South Carolina

PENNSYLVANIA
MARYLAND
Baltimore
Annapolis
OHIO
WEST VIRGINIA
WASHINGTON, D.C.
Charleston
Richmond
Norfolk
KENTUCKY
VIRGINIA
Raleigh
TENNESSEE
NORTH CAROLINA
Atlantic Ocean
Columbia
SOUTH CAROLINA
Charleston
GEORGIA

Baltimore is the largest city in Maryland.
It is an important shipbuilding center.

What was the Trail of Tears?

The Cherokee were civilized Native Americans living peacefully in South Carolina with farms and schools and their own written language. But the whites could not tolerate living with them. The whites forced the Cherokee out of their homes and drove them west. Many of them died on route, on the Trail of Tears.

Where can a wild turkey find refuge?

Wild turkeys used to flourish in South Carolina, but over the years they were hunted almost to extinction. Now there is a turkey refuge in South Carolina in the Francis Marion National Forest. Here turkeys are bred and released into the wild. As a result of this breeding program, the state-wide population of wild turkeys has grown dramatically.

How did John Brown die for human rights?

JOHN BROWN WAS A LEADER IN THE FIGHT AGAINST SLAVERY. IN 1859 HE AND A party of 21 men attacked a federal arsenal (weapons store) at Harper's Ferry, West Virginia. He wanted the weapons to liberate slaves. Brown and his courageous men took hostage the 60 soldiers stationed in the arsenal. The U.S. Marines were sent against them and Brown's men surrendered, but only after two of his sons had been killed. Brown was tried and hanged for inciting rebellion, and for treason and murder.

What was the Dred Scott Case?

Dred Scott, a slave, lived for a time in the slave state of Missouri and then in the free state of Wisconsin. In 1857 Scott claimed he was free man. The Supreme Court decided against him. It also decided that slavery was legal everywhere in the U.S. This case was one of the causes of the Civil War.

Which megastar had his home at Memphis?

BORN IN TUPELO, MISSISSIPPI, ELVIS PRESLEY MOVED TO MEMPHIS, TENNESSEE, AS A teenager. When he became a superstar he bought Graceland, a mansion just outside the town. He lived there with his wife, and then during the years that he spent alone. It was at Graceland that he died of heart failure in 1977. The mansion is now a site of pilgrimage for his millions of fans. Elvis was the highest-paid performer in the history of show business.

Elvis Presley is probably the most famous entertainer of the 20th century.

What was the "monkey trial"?

In the early years of this century a biologist named Charles Darwin claimed that people were descended from apes. This upset the Church, which taught that Adam and Eve were our first ancestors. The Church was very strong in the state of Tennessee, and a law was passed there making it illegal to teach Darwin's theories in schools. But in the early 1920s John Scopes, a biology teacher in Dayton, Tennessee, began to tell his students that people were descended from apes. In 1925 he was charged with breaking the law and fined $100 in a famous trial that became known as the "monkey trial."

When can a horse win a crown in Kentucky?

The most important and popular event of the year in Kentucky is the Kentucky Derby, which is part of the Triple Crown in the horse-racing calendar. The first Derby was run in 1867 at Churchill Downs in Louisville, Kentucky.

Where can you visit a diamond mine?

The only state in the U.S. to have produced diamonds is Arkansas, which has a diamond on its flag. Diamonds were first discovered there in 1906. Today the Crater of Diamonds State Park is open to the public. It is the only diamond mine in the world to admit visitors.

Why are Fulbright students always on the move?

The Fulbright scholarship is an exchange program that helps American students to study abroad and students from overseas to study in America. It is open to graduates, and was started by Senator J. William Fulbright of Arkansas in 1946. From 1966 teachers and researchers could also apply for study grants.

Who named Kentucky paradise?

Daniel Boone was a famous pioneer and hunter in the early days of American settlement. He loved the Kentucky countryside, where he saw herds of buffalo roaming across the plains, vast tracts of forest alive with deer and wild turkeys, and rivers full of fish. To him Kentucky was a hunter's paradise.

Where was the most violent earthquake ever recorded in the U.S.?

At New Madrid, Missouri, in the winter of 1811 to 1812. The quake registered from Canada to the Gulf of Mexico and there were 1,874 aftershocks. Although the quake measured 8.4 on the Richter scale, fortunately very few people were killed.

Kentucky

Missouri

Why is Kentucky named the Bluegrass State?

ALTHOUGH KENTUCKY'S MAJOR CROPS ARE HEMP AND TOBACCO IT IS

known as the Bluegrass State after the great high stands of bluish-colored grasses that grow around the Lexington/ Lafayette area.

IOWA

ILLINOIS

INDIANA

OHIO

KANSAS

Jefferson City
St. Louis

Louisville

Frankfort

WEST VIRGINIA

VIRGINIA

MISSOURI

KENTUCKY

Knoxville

NORTH CAROLINA

Nashville

OKLAHOMA

ARKANSAS

Memphis

TENNESSEE

GEORGIA

ALABAMA

Little Rock

MISSISSIPPI

Tennessee

TEXAS

LOUISIANA

Arkansas

The Gateway Arch in St. Louis is a memorial to the pioneers of the West.

HAWAII

What happened to Captain Cook in Hawaii?

In 1778 Captain Cook arrived in Hawaii and named the islands the Sandwich Islands after his sponsor, the Earl of Sandwich. He got on well with the islanders until 1779, when they quarreled over the theft of one of the Captain's boats. Going ashore to recover his boat from the thief, Cook was ambushed in a fight and killed.

Hawaii

Honolulu

Pacific Ocean

What was the worst natural disaster in U.S. history?

In 1992, Hurricane Andrew hit the coast of Florida and devastated Florida City and a town named Homestead. It then went on to the Gulf Coast states, where Morgan City and Lafayette in Louisiana suffered terrible damage. In all, Hurricane Andrew caused $20 billion worth of damage and left an estimated 40 dead.

Where did people live in a cave for 8,000 years?

The Russell Caves near Bridgeport, Alabama, extend miles into the mountainside. The cave closest to the entrance shows signs that humans must have lived there for over 8,000 years. The caves were declared a national monument in 1961.

Which town does Oprah Winfrey call home?

OPRAH WINFREY WAS BORN IN KOSCIUSKO, MISSISSIPPI, IN 1954, and began her TV career as a co-anchor on the evening news at Nashville TV. By 1978 she had moved on to talk shows and soon hosted her own Oprah Winfrey Show. She will talk about absolutely anything, which has made her enormously popular. She has her own production company and has starred in two movies, *The Color Purple*, for which she was nominated for an Oscar, and *Beloved*. The Oprah Winfrey Show is seen all over the world.

Why do people flock to Florida?

Over 5,000 people move to Florida each year. It has more newcomers than any other state and the fourth biggest population in the U.S.. Many newcomers are retired people who move there to enjoy the sunshine. Many others are refugees from Cuba or Haiti seeking work.

Who erected a monument to a boll weevil?

The boll weevil is a bug that eats the heart of the cotton seed, destroying the crop. Many southern states grew nothing but cotton until 1915, when a plague of boll weevils ate everything and forced them to grow different things. Although 1915 was a disaster for the farmers, when they grew more crops in following years, they were better off. So in gratitude, the farmers of Enterprise, Alabama, erected a monument to the boll weevil.

The Mississippi River was used as a major transport route by Union forces in the Civil War.

Alabama

Where do trees have their roots in the air?

THE EVERGLADES NATIONAL PARK IN FLORIDA IS A VAST SALTWATER swamp full of mangrove trees. It gets its magical name because it seems like an endless expanse of green glades. Mangrove trees thrive in tidal salt water. When the tide goes out, their roots are exposed to the air. Alligators bask in the swamp and the trees are home to spoonbills, brown pelicans, ospreys, and bald eagles.

Georgia

Florida

Cape Canaveral, Florida

Louisiana

Mississippi

Who wrote about a mockingbird?

Harper Lee was born in Monroeville, Alabama. Although she studied law, she became an airline ticket clerk before quitting her job to become a writer. Her novel *To Kill A Mockingbird* won the Pulitzer Prize in 1961 and was made into a movie starring Gregory Peck. It is about the trial of an innocent black man.

Who were the first Americans to shoot briefly into space?

Cape Canaveral in Florida is America's major launch site for most of its space exploration projects. In 1961 Alan Shepard took off from here on the first manned American flight. It was suborbital and lasted 15 minutes. The following year, John Glenn became the first American to orbit the earth. His flight lasted just 4 minutes 55 seconds.

Which Dayton brothers pioneered air travel?

THE WRIGHT BROTHERS MADE THEIR FIRST POWERED FLIGHT IN NORTH CAROLINA, but they lived and designed their planes in Dayton, Ohio. The brothers lived together all their lives and enjoyed mechanics from a very young age. They opened a bicycle repair shop and also made their own bicycles. It was a short leap from bicycles to gliders. They built their first glider in 1900 and went on to construct the first manned powered airplane.

What was the worst air disaster in the U.S.?
In 1979 an engine fell off a DC 10 as it was taking off from O' Hare Airport, Chicago. The plane flew out of control and crashed. All 273 people on board were killed.

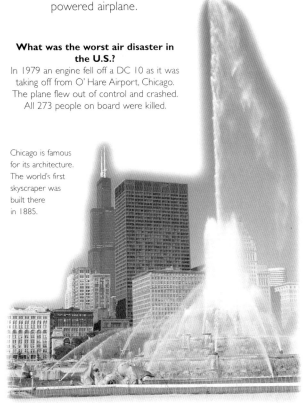

Chicago is famous for its architecture. The world's first skyscraper was built there in 1885.

How did Toni win world recognition?
Toni Morrison grew up in Lorain, Ohio and attended Harvard and Cornell Universities. Her novel *Beloved* won the 1987 Pulitzer Prize and in 1993 she won the Nobel Prize for Literature.

Why was Anthony Wayne mad?
Mad Anthony Wayne was an early pioneer who got his nickname when he stormed a British fort in a surprise night attack. He fought against the Native Americans in the Battle of Fallen Timbers, and helped drive them out of their homelands in Ohio, Indiana, Michigan, and Illinois.

Why did Ohio and Michigan nearly go to war?
Ohio and Michigan both claimed they owned an area around Toledo. In 1836 the two states called out their armies and were ready to fight. Then Congress gave the area to Ohio—and it gave Michigan some land in the Upper Peninsula. So both states were happy again.

What made Sarah Breedlove rich?
Born in 1867 in Louisiana, Sarah Breedlove invented a formula for straightening curly hair. She began by selling her product from door to door in 1905. Her business grew and she opened the Madam C. Walker Manufacturing Company in Indianapolis. Sarah Breedlove was the first black American woman in the U.S. to become a millionaire.

Where is America's largest prison?
Mississippi. Its State Penitentiary is the largest in America with a total of 1,536 inmates. Ohio has the second largest Federal Correctional Institute in the U.S. with a population of 47,248, then comes Michigan Federal Correctional Institution with 43,784 residents, and then Illinois with 40,425.

Michigan

Ohio

WISCONSIN

Lake Michigan

Lansing

CANADA

Lake Erie

Detroit

Illinois

ILLINOIS

IOWA

Chicago

Toledo

Cleveland

PENNSYLVANIA

OHIO

ILLINOIS

Indianapolis

Columbus

WEST VIRGINIA

Springfield

INDIANA

Cincinnati

Indiana

MISSOURI

KENTUCKY

Who is Steveland Judkins Morris?

He is better known as Stevie Wonder. He was born blind in Saginaw, Michigan, in 1950. By age 13 he had his own recording contract and was known as "Little Stevie Wonder." During the 1970s and 1980s he produced many smash hits, recording them in Detroit on the Tamla Motown record label.

One of Stevie Wonder's biggest hits was *Superstition*.

Who was the first woman to run for presidency of the U.S.?

VICTORIA CLAFLIN WOODHULL (1838–1927) WAS BORN IN

Homer, Ohio. She was a feminist and social reformer, and the first woman to be nominated as a presidential candidate. She stood for the presidency in 1872 as a representative of the Equal Rights Party. She was not elected. She believed in equal rights, but she also supported the idea of eugenics—which means allowing only beautiful and intelligent people to have children.

Index

AB

CDE

FGH

IJKL

MNO

OPQR

STU

VWXYZ

ACKNOWLEDGEMENTS

The photographs in this book were supplied
by: Camera Press 31 (Jerzy Dabrowski; Peter
Newark's Pictures 9, 10, 19, 24, 26; Roger
Vlitos 16.